I0008952

HTML

Quick Guide

<p>Build your Web</p>

ISBN-10: 1502742314

ISBN-13: 978-1502742315

Dedication

To all of you wishing to learn HTML to build your own websites or just to learn it. I am a designer who loves art in the first place and well designed websites. It was a point in my life when I decided to pursue the path of HTML as a hoby and as a career choice simply because I enjoy creating sites from scratch keeping in mind how simple and easy to code in HTML.

I decided to write this book which is a quick guide and make it available to all of you interested in learning this Markup Language to use it in your daily life as a hobby or a career.

The choice is yours!

Table of contents:

1. <u>Introduction</u>:

HTML stands for HyperText Markup Language, widely used to write and make a web page.

HyperText: the relationship between links in a web page/pages; Hyper is not linear and you can go to any site without being obliged to follow a structured way or forced to visit a site before to get where you want to go; Text is simply a description or explanation of things.

Markup Language: basically the structure of the web page; Markup is same as editing a text it's what you do with it; Language as it uses English words.

It was meant for structuring a document to share. Very simple to use if you learn which markup to use.

Coding with HTML is easy all you need is a text editor and a web browser.

To create a web page start by the following:

Note: < > is used to open the Tag and </ >to close it and end it.

<!DOCTYPE html> DOCTYPE: indicates which version of XHTML is used, here it's html.

<html>

<head>

<title>write something</title>

</head>

<body>

<hn(n=1 to 6)>used for the heading</hn> Note: n= a number from 1 being bold and big to 6 being small text.

<p (paragraph)>...</p> You can repeat this attribute in a row many times.

</body>

```
</html>
```

Or simply by typing the below elements you've already created a web:

```
<html>
```

```
<head>...</head>
```

```
<body>...</body>
```

```
</html>
```

With the above you have already created an HTML page! All what you needed is: a Head (with some attributes such as a title) and a Body (with some attributes such as a paragraph and more…)

Note: <title>, <hn>, <p>….etc are called tags.

To create a web page you can use **NotePad**, open it then choose:

Save as: .html or .htm

Save file type: All files.

Once saved open it (right click on it, choose: open with, then the browser) and it's the web page that you'll be adding more structure and attributes to it.

Any change made in the notepad save it and go to the browser file you created and refresh or hit F5.

All the updates you made to the file will instantly appear on your web page.

We use .htm or .html as the HTML file extension.

Tags can be followed by attributes which is optional, as many as you want.

Each tag has a name placed between brackets, <Tag name> to open and

</Tag name> to close.

HTML Tags and attributes are not case sensitive, which is Not the case for XHTML.

The following are the minimum tags or elements included in HTML:

<html>, <head>, <title> (the name that appears in the browser for searching purpose) and <body>.

Note: For each opening tag above, there is a closing tag by using </...>.

2. Different Tags in HTML:

2a- Title tag <title>:

<title> element: following the <head> gives a title to the page, used in search engines and comes at the top of the browser.

(See sample title of the web page).

Sample code:

```
<html>

<head>
<title>TEST HTML</title>
</head>

<body></body>

</html>
```

See at the top it shows: TEST HTML

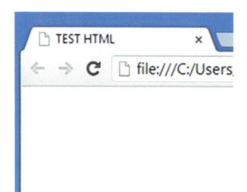

2b- <u>Paragraph tag \<p></u>:

\<body> element may contain attributes such as paragraphs \<p>...\</p>. .

Check the sample code:

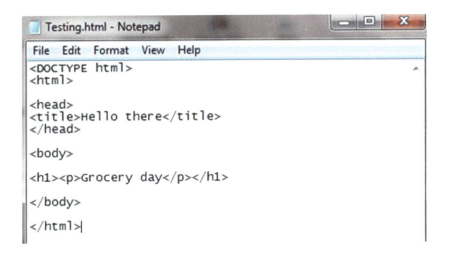

See the result:

So the browser shows the paragraph "Grocery day" very large because of the <h1> and </h1> open/close tags placed at the beginning and end of the <p>...</p> open/close tags.

The <hn></hn> tag when surrounding tags and texts gives a level of large to small text.

n= represents a number from 1 to 6, so the heading h1 being the largest text and h6 being the smallest.

Let's see the example: The elements h1, h2, h3, h4, h5 and h6 are headings.

```
Testing.html - Notepad
File  Edit  Format  View  Help
<DOCTYPE html>
<html>

<head>
<title>Hello there</title>
</head>

<body>

<h1>Just to say hi</h1>
<h2>Just to say hi</h2>
<h3>Just to say hi</h3>
<h4>Just to say hi</h4>
<h5>Just to say hi</h5>
<h6>Just to say hi</h6>

</body>

</html>
```

See the result: h1 heading to h6:

2c- Style:

 An attribute that enables adding a color background, followed by an "="
equal sign, use of semicolon to separate different style statements.

For color choices write the one you want or for more choices click on the
web link and you'll see the color code at the top, copy it adding # before it.

The color choice is from the vertical color option or by just clicking inside
the square as well.

 Please hold down ctrl and click: http://www.colorpicker.com/

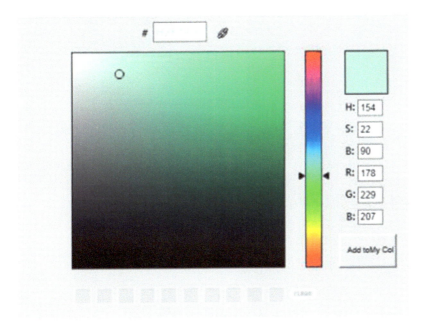

HTML sample:

```
<h3 style="background-color:blue;">Hi there</h3>
<h2 style="background-color:#ff0000;">Hi there</h2>
<h5 style="background-color:#B2E5CF;">Hi there</h5>
```

See the web result:

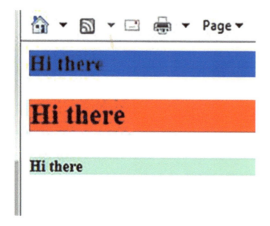

2d- **Emphasis tag <em> in HTML**:

<head> element or tag comes right after the <html> tag or element it includes the title and other attributes such as style, emphasis, a link...etc.

Sample without <em> tag:

```
<!DOCTYPE html>
<html>

<head>
<title>Hello there</title>
</head>

<body>
<p>Just asking</p>
</body>

</html>
```

Result:

Just asking

Once you add <em> and </em>, save and refresh.

See sample:

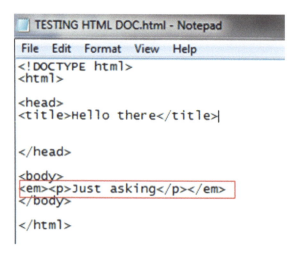

See paragraph change:

Just asking

2e- Strong tag <strong>:

<strong>…</strong> helps to outstand the important part of the text.

```
<p>Hello there</p>
<strong>Hello there</strong>
```

See the result once the strong tag added:

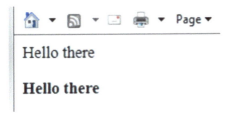

2f- <u>Break tag
</u>:

Do we need always an opening and closing tag in HTML? No not always, there are few exceptions, few elements open and close in the same tag and are called empty elements they serve a particular purpose when used.

Example of such would be the line break tag represented by:

See sample:

```
<em><strong>we go to shop</strong></em><br/>let's go
```

The result is:

As you can see the <br /> breaks the two texts into two lines.

Also you can use more than one element on the same line <em> and <strong> tags were simultaneously used, as long as it's not too crowded. You can also see that by using <strong></strong> around a text it makes it bold.

Another example for <br /> tag:

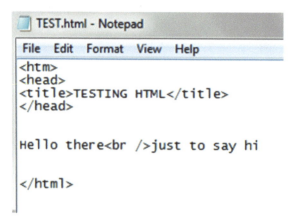

Result:

2g- Horizontal tag <hr />:

Another element on its own is the <hr /> , hr is an abbreviation for: horizontal line.

See sample:

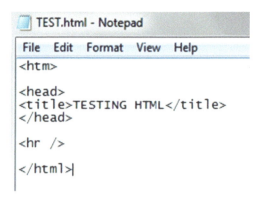

The result shows a horizontal line.

2h- Lists:

Lists has an open and a closed tags such as <ul> </ul>, <ol> </ol> and

<li> </li>.

Li stands for list, ul is for unordered lists and ol for the ordered ones (numbering them).

<ol> </ol> makes all enclosed items stated in the <li> </li> in an ordered list.

Check the sample:

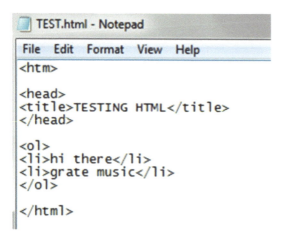

Check the browser result:

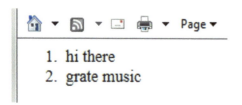

While using the <ul> </ul> (unordered list) tags bullets are added to the enclosed texts in <li> </li>.

Sample code:

```
<ul>
<li>hi there</li>
<li>good music</li>
</ul>
```

See web page result:

- hi there
- good music

2i- **Definition list tag:**

<dl> </dl> tags stand for definition list, <dt> </dt> for definition term and <dd > </dd> for the definition of the term.

See sample of all the 3 tags:

```
File   Edit   Format   View   Help
<html>

<head>
<title>TESTING HTML</title>
</head>

<body>

<dl>
 <dt>Bread</dt>
   <dd>Food made of flour, water and yeast</dd>
 <dt>Muffin</dt>
   <dd>a small domed cake or quick bread made from
     butter or dough</dd>
</dl>

</body>

</html>
```

Result:

> Bread
>   Food made of flour, water and yeast
> Muffin
>   a small domed cake or quick bread made from butter or dough

2j- Delete and Insert tags:

We can add the <del>...</del> tags that deletes part of the paragraph combined with the <ins>…</ins> tags for the new inserted part.

See sample:

```
<html>

<head>
<title>TESTING HTML</title>
</head>

<body>

<p>I love <del>chicken</del> <ins>veggie</ins> pitzza!</p>

</body>

</html>
```

Check the result:

I love ~~chicken~~ <u>veggie</u> pitzza!

2k- Text Elements:

<font attributes>...</font> includes size, face and color of the enclosed text.

Note:
 tag is one of them.

Sample:

```
<body>

<font size="3" font face="Goudy Stout"
     color="blue">I love pitzza!</font> <br />

<font size="6" color="green">I love pitzza!</font> <br />

<font size="4" font face="CityBlueprint" color="green">
    I love pitzza!</font>

</body>
```

Result:

2l- Center and Italic tags:

Other text tags are: the **<center>…</center>** open/close tags to center the element **<i>…</i>** to have the text in Italic.

Sample code:

```
<body>

<p><cite>Pinocchio</cite> by Carlo Collodi. Made in 1883.</p>
<center><p><cite>Pinocchio</cite> By Carlo Collodi.
          Made in 1883.</p></center>

<i>Made in 1883</i>

</body>
```

Browser result:

Pinocchio by Carlo Collodi. Made in 1883.

Pinocchio By Carlo Collodi. Made in 1883.

Made in 1883

2m- Quotation tag:

We use <q>…</q> open/close tags for short sections to quote instead of longer ones enclosed in <blockquote> tag.

Sample code:

```
<p>Heat worning:
<q>Attract attention to the heat danger</q>
we hope to find a solution.</p>
```

Result:

Heat worning: "Attract attention to the heat danger" we hope to find a solution.

2n- **Strike tag <s>:**

<s>…</s> open/close tags were used to strike the text similar to what <strike> tag does when the text is no longer relevant or needed.

Different from the delete tag (<del>…</del>), might still working for some browsers as it worked for me using Notepad and Chrome web.

Sample code:

```
<p><s>It is nice today.</s></p>
<p>It is not nice today.</p>
```

Result of this code:

~~It is nice today.~~

It is not nice today.

2o- **Superscript and Subscript tags:**

[…] tags are used to show part of the text above the line and as you can see from sample below the word can be rendered in a smaller font. On the other hand the _… tags are used to subscript the text and make a portion of it below the line.

Sample 1 for <sup> tag:

```
<p>This table is <sup>glass</sup> table.</p>
```

Result:

This table is ^{glass} table.

Sample 2 for <sub> tag:

```
<p>This table is <sub>glass</sub> table.</p>
```

Result:

This table is ₉ₗₐₛₛ table.

2p- Variable Tag:

<var>...</var> tags and in between ... is a phrase tag, still can be used but better use CSS to get better result.

It is similar to other phrase tags such as <em> and <strong>.

Sample:

```
<var>Holiday</var>
```

Result:

Holiday

2q- Bold, Big and Underlined Tags:

Bold tag:

<b>...</b> open/close tags make the text bold, but in HTML5 we should consider to use first the headings "h1, h2, ...h6" or <strong> before thinking to use the bold tag.

Big tag:

<big>…</big> tag is used to make the text bigger.

Underline tag:

<u>…</u> tag used to make a part of the text stands out because it's different than the rest of it.

Check the sample:

```
<p><b>Opening the door</b><p>

<p><big>Opening the door</big></p>

<p><u>Opening</u> the door</p>
```

See result: <b> for bold, **<big>** for big and **<u>** for underline.

Opening the door

Opening the door

Opening the door

3. **More tags and Attributes**: Important for html, each tag has its own attributes.

3a- **Image tag and attributes:**

img tag stands for image and has 2 required attributes: "src" and "alt".

Images are linked to HTML.

By simply nesting <img> tag inside <a> tag we can link an image to another document.

using: src (abbreviation for source), width, hight, title, valign, border...etc.

<img src="image URL" attr_name="attr_value"/>

You can add more attribute names as mentioned above such as "hight", "width"...etc in the <img src="url"...="..."/> tag.

The image can be: GIF, JPEG or PNG.

Go to the browser and type in Skype, select images from the top, click on "view image" then copy the link from the browser of that image and paste it as an "image URL" after <img src="....Or choose any image you like.

See **sample code**: (Skype is used just to demonstrate an HTML tag, so no commercial purpose, it can be any other image instead).

```
<body>

<img src="http://www.skypeassets.com/i/common/images/icons/
skype-logo-open-graph.png" alt="skype logo" height="100"
width="150" />

</body>
```

Browser result:

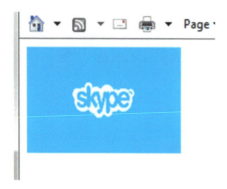

Note: When selecting images from the web, click on "Search tools", and under "Usage rights" choose "Labeled for reuse" Or "Labeled for reuse with modification".

The best is to search for **free images** to use for learning or any purposes.

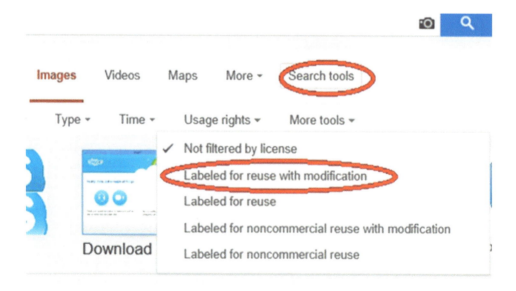

Another way to use <img..../> tag is just by simply typing the name of the picture you saved in your computer, an example would be to save a picture from the web or your camera to your desktop (ensure that the picture is in the same location of the .html document you are working on otherwise it will not work).

If your .html document is somewhere else other than the desktop, the picture has to be there as well (same path, same folder).

See sample code and result for an image:

```
<body>
<div align="center">
<img src="Butterfly.jpg" hight=500" width=200"/>
</div>
</body>
```

Result:

Note: you don't have to use the <div>...</div> tag but using it in the <div align="center">...</div> and wrapping the <img.../> into a <div> element allows you to take advantage of the CSS styles instead of coding.

3b- <u>Image link (Hyperlink)</u>:

The <a> tag defines a hyperlink that links one page to another , it uses the href attribute for the link's destination, any URL (Uniform Resource Locator) which is a web address when using http the protocol identifier.

The image link comes often automatically with border that you can get rid of by typing "border 0 or 1" inside the <img src="…" border="0 or 1" /> tag at the end.

See example:

```
<a href="http://butterflywebsite.com/">
<img src="Apolloo2s.gif"/>
</a>
```

Result:

Click on the picture added and it will take you to the web page.

By adding a paragraph, and choosing a specific position for it or not you can have as well a link to click on instead of the image.

Check the code:

```
<a href="http://butterflywebsite.com"/>
<img src="Apollo2.gif"/>
<left><p>The Apollo Butterfly</p></left>
</a>
```

Result:

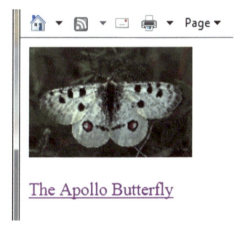

The Apollo Butterfly

In this case you can click either on: the purple link or the picture.

Try a sample yourself.

3c- **Thumbnails type**:

Also the most common image link used nowadays is the thumbnails type.

Its purpose is for quick reviews very useful for image gallery and allows browser to load faster. Not smaller than 75x75 pixels.

Here is how to create a thumbnail picture, simply right click on it, choose

edit, once in paint : choose image, then choose "Resize and Skew".

In the Resize part enter 5% (for example) in the horizontal box and the vertical automatically fills 5.

Save the image as…(give it a name)

To find it later, go to your html document and add it to your:

<img src="….jpg"> and of course the <a href="http…"> is already there.

Save the html file and refresh your browser then click on the link, you will see the picture in its full resolution.

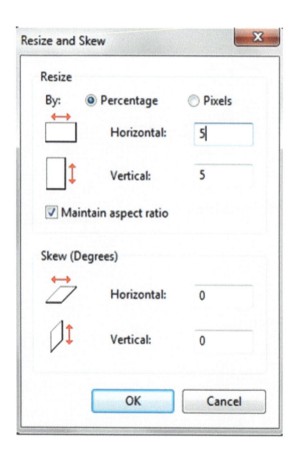

Sample:

```
<a href="http://butterflywebsite.com"/>
<img src="Apolloo2s resized.gif"/>
</a>
```

Result:

Click on the small picture when you try the sample yourself.

4. HTML Tables:

Tables are still widely used, it starts with an opening <table> tag or <tb> and ends with a closing </tb> tag, it's made of rows <tr> and columns or data cells <td> enclosed in the <tr>...</tr> tags.

<table border="n"> to open and </table> to close, n is a number like 1.

<tr> tag for row, enclosed in the table tag.

<td> tag for column, enclosed in the table row tag.

See sample:

```
<html>
<head>
<title>TEST</title>
</head>

<body>
<table border="1" cellspacing="2" cellpadding="3">

<tr><th>Nancy</th><th>Betty</th><th>Donald</th></tr>

<tr>
<td>February</td><td>Butterfly</td><td>March</td>
</tr>

<tr>
<td>Earth</td><td>Sun</td><td>Mars</td>
</tr>

</table>
</body>
</html>
```

Result:

Nancy	Betty	Donald
February	Butterfly	March
Earth	Sun	Mars

We can use an image instead of a text.

See sample:

```
<html>
<head>
<title>TEST</title>
</head>

<body>
<table border="1" cellspacing="2" cellpadding="3">

<tr><th>Nancy</th><th>Betty</th><th>Donald</th></tr>

<tr>
<td>February</td>
<td><img src="Apollo02S.gif" alt="Butterfly"></td>
<td>March</td>
</tr>

<tr>
<td>Earth</td><td>Sun</td><td>Mars</td>
</tr>

</table>
</body>
</html>
```

Column 2, row 2 is replaced by a picture.

Nancy	Betty	Donald
February		March
Earth	Sun	Mars

We can change the border number, the cellspacing or the cellpadding numbers, but it's better to keep the table border and cells simple unless you need to do so.

See the sample:

```
<table border="9" cellspacing="7" cellpadding="14">
```

Result:

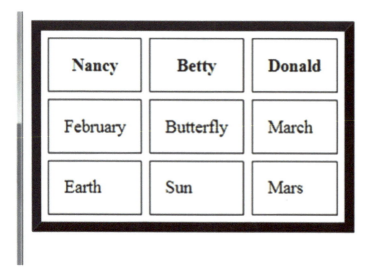

border="9" is too thick and dark.

4a- <u>**Other samples of tables**</u>:

By adding <br/> you can space the 2 tables, you can also add more attributes to the table to specify width and hight, cellpadding, specific cell color instead of a row color background, style and font, left and right cells…etc.

```
<body>
<table border="1" cellspacer=2 bgcolor="blue">
<tr>
<td>table1</td>
</tr>
</table>

<br />

<table border="3" cellspacer=5 bgcolor="red">
<tr>
<td>table2</td>
</tr>
</table>

</body>
```

Result:

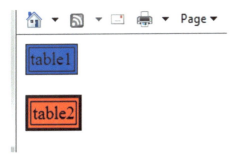

See the 2 tables **without <br /> tag**:

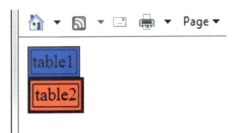

5. Comment tag in HTML:

Comments are invisible or ignored by the web and start with:

<!-- Write what you want here -->

Where <!-- is the opening tag and --> the closing one.

Very useful to keep up with history changes, modifications made, notes etc...

Sample: <!-- display a butterfly picture --> then follow by adding an image,

Sample image: <img src="flower2.jpg" hight="250" width="150"/>.

Note: the code file and the image should be in the same folder or path for the picture to appear.

```
<html>
<title>TEST</title>

<body>

<!-- display a butterfly picture -->
<img src="flower2.jpg" hight="250" width="150"/>

</body>
</html>
```

Result:

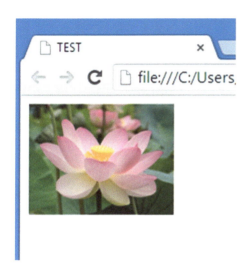

6. **<u>Background color or bgcolor attribute</u>**:

It is used to control the background of the body element and the table or any tag, basically it changes the HTML page's background color.

The tag to use is the following: <tagname bgcolor="color_value"...>.

Even if it is an easy and a simple attribute to use it is still depreciated in HTML5 and its usage is discouraged, in CSS all styling is done trough style sheet.

Sample:

```
<!DOCTYPE html>
<html>
<head>
<title>TEST</title>
</head>
<body bgcolor="red">
<p>let's go to the store</p>

</body>
</html>
```

The result:

let's go to the store

You can use the coloring code instead, go to www.colorpicker.com and choose a code color that you need, example: #F51448 for a different type of red.

See sample code:

```
<!DOCTYPE html>
<html>
<head>
<title>TEST</title>
</head>

<body bgcolor="#F51448">

<p>Let's go to the store</p>

</body>
</html>
```

Result:

For tables: we have seen it already (please check previous samples) and here is one more sample:

```
<!DOCTYPE html>
<html>
<head>
<title>TEST</title>
</head>
<body>

<table bgcolor="pink" width="100%">
<tr>
<td>pink is my favorite color</td>
</tr>
</table>

</body>
</html>
```

Result:

pink is my favorite color

7. Adding Videos in HTML:

The minimum tag you need to open a video in HTML is:<embed src="name of the file">.

Or instead copy the URL from the video you like.

If it is a YouTube video, look for Share below the video and copy the URL from there or simply from the above URL link.

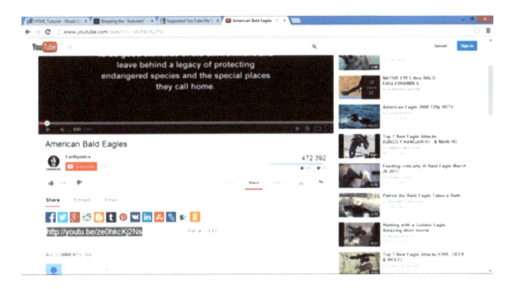

Note: the video file and the code file (Notpad in my case with extention .html) have to be in the same folder or directory to work (if the 2 files are saved in different places it will not work) to solve this you have to add the path or the location of the file in the code.

Do not forget to write the extension file name example: .mp4 or .mp3 or....in the code.

If you do not want your video to start right away once open in the browser add: **autostart="false"** /> to <embed src="name of the file".

BUT in my case not having a media player or any MP3 ... I found that the easiest way to add a YouTube video is by using the "**iframe tag**"

Example:

<iframe width="..." height="..." src="URL" frameborder="0" allowfullscreen></iframe> that you can copy from below the video you have chosen.

Select "Share" that you find below the video then EMBED , copy the URL from the rectangular area that opens, after pasting it as it is in your Notepad .html file make corrections to it.

See corrections made to the iframe code below:

When copied from EMBED (check the highlighted part):

<iframe width="560" height="315" src="//www.youtube.com/embed/r3w4nh48oBU" frameborder="0" allowfullscreen></iframe>

After corrections made (check the highlighted part):

<iframe width="560" height="315" src="http://youtube.com/embed/r3w4nh48oBU" frameborder="0" allowfullscreen></iframe>

7a- **Sample #1 use of EMBED Tag:**

```
<html>
<title>TEST</title>

<body>

<embed width="360" height="290"
src="American Bald Eagles.MP4"
autostart="false" />


</body>

</html>
```

Result:

7b- **Sample #2 use of IFRAME Tag:**

```
<html>

<head>
<title>TESTING HTML</title>
</head>

<body>

<iframe width="420" height="315"
src="//www.youtube.com/embed/ze0hkcKj2Ns"
frameborder="0" allowfullscreen></iframe>

</body>

</html>
```

Result:

8. Script in HTML:

Add the <script> open tag and </sript> close tag between the open/close head tags.

Then write whatever you want: <scrip>alert("...");</script>.

In this sample I used: HELLO THERE!!!

Do not forget to put ; after you finish your alert word or sentence.

Check the code:

```
<html>
<head>
<title>TEST</title>

<script>
alert("HELLO THERE!!!");
</script>

</head>

<body>

DO SOME SHOPPING

</body>

</html>
```

Result:

If you click OK the text DO SOME SHOPPING will appear.

You can put if you wish the script tag in the body part, therefore the text: DO SOME SHOPPING will appear fist and the alert box next but it is so fast that it seems they appear (text and box) at the same time.

See a sample code:

```
<body>

DO SOME SHOPPING

<script>
alert("HELLO THERE!!!");
</script>

</body>
```

9. Audio in HTML:

<embed src="....mp3 or mp4"/> is just a simple code for audio in HTML.

You can add the size, the loop if you want your audio to start again automatically or not by just entering the values true or false.

Usually when we put "autostart="false" not "true" that means we do not want the audio to start right away until we click on start button, but in chrome's browser for example it will not stop playing or wait until you click on start, that is why we need to add in the code: **type**="audio/?" and the ? means you need to specify the type of the file that the browser is dealing with and in our sample it was an mp4 file.

See sample:

```
<html>

<head>
<title>TESTING HTML</title>
</head>

<body>

<embed src="Beautiful Day- U2 Lyrics.mp3" width="300"
height="250" autostart="false" type="audio/mp4"
loop="false" volume="40" />

<p>Please choose stop/pause.</p>

</body>

</html>
```

If this appear:

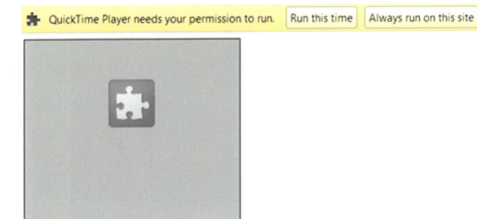

Please choose stop pause.

Click on Run this time, an audio bar appear, see the result:

Please choose stop/pause.

Without adding **TYPE** in the code:

```
<body>

<embed src="Beautiful Day- U2 Lyrics.mp3" width="300"
height="250" autostart="false" loop="false"
volume="40" />

<p>Please choose stop/pause.</p>

</body>
```

Result: The audio will start immediately even stating in your code: autostart="false".

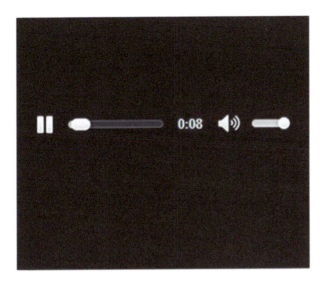

Please choose stop/pause.

10. Pre code (tag) in HTML:

Pre code in HTML: <pre>...</pre> are the open/close tags.

Use it for any special occasions, wherever you want to keep your text the way you typed it, keeping its line breaks spaces etc...

Sample code:

```
<html>
<head>
<title>TEST</title>

</head>

<body>

<pre>
let's check for shoes
        Blue or red
                that's the color I like
If you prefer another color please say so!!! :)
</pre>

</body>

</html>
```

The result in the browser:

```
let's check for shoes
        Blue or red
                that's the color I like
If you prefer another color please say so!!! :)
```

11. Div code (tag) in HTML:

Uses <div>...</div> the open/close tags.

The <div> tag can contain many tags such as <font>, <a>, <small>, <table> and so on...

The <div> tag is used to identify sections and works with CSS , and can be used to group any elements, it acts as a block element, it can be used for example with "id" for web sections identification.

The <div> tag can contain any elements you pick, it doesn't have a precise content.

Sample:

```
<html>

<head>
<title>TESTING HTML</title>
</head>

<body>

<div id="menuPane">
  <div class="menu">
   <h2>Site Info</h2>

    <a href="http://www.skype.com/" >Home</a>
    For support click on:
    <a href="https://support.skype.com/en/" > Support</a>

  </div>

  <div class="menu">
    <h3> For rates and prices check the link</h3>
    <a href="http://www.skype.com/en/rates/" > Rates</a>
  </div>

</body>

</html>
```

Result:

Here we used the <a> tag with the <div> one, the texts highlighted are links.

Site Info

Home For support click on: Support

For rates and prices check the link

Rates

12. **Meta Tags in HTML:**

Are codes placed in the head section (header) in html document, they contain description, keywords owner, title, author's information , language and other important information about your webpage.

Each meta tag provides search engines SEO (search engine optimization) with a specific information to help properly rank and find faster your website.

The <Meta > tag is a little different than the other tags we use in HTML .

The <Meta> tags are between the open/close <head> </head> tags, check the sample code.

The two (2) meta tags, description and keywords are the minimum tags to use.

Name is used to identify the meta tag and content is to define things related to the tag.

Other Meta tags sample:

<meta name="copyright" content="enter details here ...the year">

<meta name="rating" content="enter the rating here">

<meta name="author" content="enter the name here">

Note: Make sure to enter unique keywords that work the best for what your webpage is about.

```
<html>

<head>
<title>TESTING HTML</title>
</head>

<body>

<meta name="description" content="this is about....">
<meta name="keywords" content="flowers, new, description,
              training">

</head>

<body>

<p>Today is a nice day</p>

</body>

</html>
```

13. **Password field in HTML:**

The password is set by using the <input> tag and specifying a value.

Check sample code:

```
<html>

<head>
<title>TESTING HTML</title>
</head>

<body>

<form>
Password <input type="password" title="user login"
          maxlength="4">
<input type="submit" name="Submit">
</form>

</body>

</html>
```

Result:

Password [   ] [Submit]

14. Input Code in HTML:

Which can be a check box or button, reset, password etc...

Check sample code:

```
<html>
<head>
<title>TEST</title>
</head>

<body>

<form name="TEST" >
   Check Here: <input type="checkbox" /><br />
   Title: <input type="text" /><br />
   Yes: <input type="checkbox" /> No: <input type="radio" />
            Maybe: <input type="radio" /><br />
   <input type="submit" value="SUBMIT" />
   <input type="reset" value="RESET" />
</form>


</body>

</html>
```

Result:

Check Here: ☐
Title: [_____]
Yes: ☐ No: ○ Maybe: ○
[SUBMIT] [RESET]

15. Text Field in HTML:

It uses the <input> tag, with the purpose of focusing on one word or a sentence.

"Name"and "id" are used for that purpose.

Sample:

```
<html>

<head>
<title>TESTING HTML</title>
</head>

<body>

<form name="TEST" >
First: <input title="Address" id="first" name="Address"
            type="text" /> <br />

Second: <input title="Zip code" id="Second"
            name="Zip code" type="text" /> <br />

<input type="SUBMIT" value="SUBMIT" />
</form>

</body>

</html>
```

Result:

First: [   ]   Second: [   ]
[SUBMIT]

If you prefer to put them on a different line you could use <br /> tag after each input.

See sample result:

First:
Second:
SUBMIT

16. **Layouts using tables in HTML:**

Tables are the best example in this case as they contain texts.

Assigning height and width to the tables need to be presize otherwise you will not get what you intended to do in the first place.

It takes a little practice to get adjusted to knowing exactly what to do.

1st sample:

```
<body>
<div style="width:30%">
<div style="background-color:grey; height:30px;
          width:100%">

<h2>TEST LAYOUTs</h2>
</div>

<div style="background-color:pink; height:150px;
          width:85px; float:left;">
    <div><b>Check below</b></div>
    Sound<br />
</div>

<div style="background-color:blue; height:150px;
          width:150px; float:left;">
<p>Just for testing purpose</p>
</div>

<div style="background-color:orange; height:150px;
          width:70px; float:right;">
<div><b>Check</b></div>
    Price...<br />type<br />
</div>
<div style="background-color:red; height:150px;
          width:100px; float:right;">
    <div><h3><b>Above</p></b></h3></div>
</div>
</body>
```

Result:

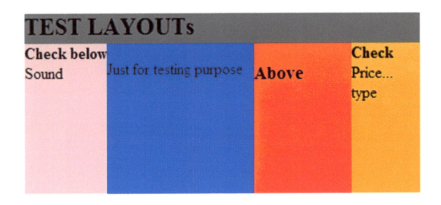

2nd sample:

```
<html>
<head>
<title>TEST</title>
</head>

<body>

<table id="1st" border="0" bgcolor="red" height="100" width="200">
<tr>
<td>

<table id="2nd" border="0" bgcolor="blue" height="70" width="90">
<tr>
<td>

<table id="3rd" bgcolor="yellow" height="50" width="70">
<tr>
<td>

</tr>
</table>
</td>
</tr>
</table>

</body>

</html>
```

<u>Result:</u>

<u>3rd sample for Layouts:</u>

```
<body>

<table cellspacing="0" cellpadding="0" border="3"
        id="outline" height="200" width="300">
<tr height="50">
<td colspan="3" bgcolor="white">
<table title="TEST  border="3">
<tr><td>Testing table</td></tr>
</table>

<tr height="150">
<td bgcolor="yellow">

<table id="menue1" border="0">
<tr><td>TB1</td></tr>
<tr><td>TB2</td></tr>
</table>

<td bgcolor="red">
<table id="menue2" border="0">
<tr><td>TB3</td></tr>
<tr><td>TB4</td></tr>
</table>

<td bgcolor="gray">
<table id="menue3" border="3">
<tr><td>TB5</td></tr>
<tr><td>TB6</td></tr>
</table>

</body>
```

Result:

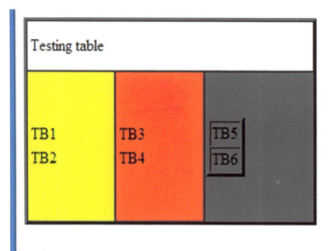

17. <u>Textarea tag in HTML</u>:

Its purpose is creating a form to write a content similar to a field that can be sized.

The text can be arranged in rows and columns which determines the number of characters per line.

Check the sample code:

```
<html>
<head>
<title>TEST</title>
</head>

<body>

<form>

<textarea name="Description" cols="15" rows="5">
This is just a sample text to show the texarea code
and its use and also the sizing and also ...</textarea>

</form>


</body>

</html>
```

See result:

```
This is just    ^
a sample text
to show the
texarea code    v
and its use and
```

18. Email tag in HTML:

Use <a href> tag for Email links, which is a standard <a> tag and an 'href ' added.

Check sample code ,"mailto:sample@gmail.com"> Then before closing tag </a>.

Write for example: Email me please, which will be highlighted in the end to click on.

It is very important to have an email address in most cases for clients to contact you.

```
<html>
<head>
<title>TEST</title>
</head>

<body>

<a href="mailto:sample@gmail.com">Contact me</a>

</body>

</html>
```

Result:

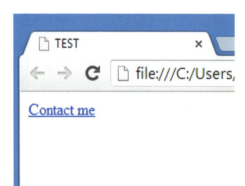

19. Copyright in HTML:

It is part of the Entities.

Enter: &copy to make "©" Copyright symbol.

Sample code:

```
<html>
<head>
<title>TEST</title>
</head>

<body>

<p> &copy makes Copyright symbol.</p>

</body>

</html>
```

Result:

© makes Copyright symbol.

20. HTML Entities sample:

Check few HTML entities , each character has a corresponding entity number and sometimes name as well, they are used when needed while coding in HTML, there are many more then listed.

Footnotes: Referencing may be used at the bottom of the page in texts, Superscript tags can be used for this purpose in HTML.

```
<body>

<p> &#37 for Percent sign </p>
<p> &#38 for Ampersand, or use entity name
    instead: &amp </p>
<p> &#60 for less than, or use entity name
    instead: &lt </p>
<p> &#62 for greater than, or use entity name
    instead: &gt </p>
<p> &#64 for At sign</p>
<p> &#126 for Tilde </p>
<p> &#162 for Cent, or use entity name
    instead: &cent </p>
<p> &#174 for Registered trademark, or use
    entity name instead: &reg </p>
<p> &#177 Plus or minus, or use entity name
    instead: &plusmn </p>
<p> &#178 for Superscript 2, or use entity name
    instead: &sup2 </p>
<p> &#189 for Fraction 1/2, or use entity name
    instead: &frac12 </p>
<p> &#8594 for Right arrow, or use entity name
    instead: &rarr; </p>

</body>
```

Check the result below for each paragraph's content:

% for Percent sign

& for Ampersand, or use entity name instead: &

< for less than, or use entity name instead: <

> for greater than, or use entity name instead: >

@ for At sign

~ for Tilde

¢ for Cent, or use entity name instead: ¢

® for Registered trademark, or use entity name instead: ®

± Plus or minus, or use entity name instead: ±

² for Superscript 2, or use entity name instead: ²

½ for Fraction 1/2, or use entity name instead: ½

→ for Right arrow, or use entity name instead: →

21. **Fieldset tag in HTML**:

Starts with the <fieldset> opening tag under the form tag and ends with the </fieldset> closing one located in the body section of HTML coding, they are the main tags for creating the set.

Fieldset is a set of elements under the same form in a more descriptive way, that can have a name in the legend tag if you choose to do so.

In the first sample below we used the legend called "Information" so we gave a name to the form then from there we requested a phone number and so on (information of that group is put together).

The sections in the form to check and sometimes to enter information are like labels to clarify the document and make it understandable by visual tools such as using a check boxe for example.

Please practice the samples, this is the best way to learn.

```
<!DOCTYPE html>
<html>
<head>
<title>TEST</title>
</head>
<body>

<form>
<fieldset>
<legend>Information</legend>
Phone n#: <input type="box"> Address:<input type="radio">
<br />
Postal code:<input type="text">
</fieldset>
</form> <br />
<fieldset form="My info" disabled> <legend>Details</legend>
My current assignment
</fieldset> <br />
<fieldset>
<p>Phone n#: <input type="Checkbox" style="width:90px";>
Home phone n#: <input type="text" style="width:90px";></p>
<p>Contact name: <input type="radio" style="width:30px;">
</p>
<input type="radio" name="Location" value="South"> South
<input type="radio" name="Location" value="North"> North
<input type="submit" value="SUBMIT">
<input type="reset" value="RESET">
</fieldset>

</body>
</html>
```

Result:

22. Frameset tag in HTML:

It uses the opening tag <framset> in the body section and the closing one </frameset> and acts as a document that divides the screen.

Frameset holds elements, the element specifies the layout in a rectangular way.

The rows attribute are used for horizontal frames and cols (columns) for the vertical ones.

Both can be used interchanged and we use <frame> tag to indicate the frame.

The surface of the screen differ from a device to another, therefore the usage of this tag is not advised for smaller screens which cannot be more divided.

You can divide rows or cols in % or pixels, check the sample:

The first section in rows is 70%, the second is * meaning automatically it fills the rest, but you could instead use 30% to have the 100% total .

Note: we added <frame> tag just underneath it because we had one (1) value which is the 70% If we had another one we would of added another frame tag to mach the 2 values.

For the cols (columns) we used 2 sections 10% and 90% that means we have to create 2 frames, and so on...

It is a little confusing in the beginning but practicing the code will simplify it and make it easy.

Sample:

```
<!DOCTYPE html>
<html>
<head>
<title>TEST</title>
</head>

<frameset rows="70,*">
<frame>
<frameset cols="10%,90%">
<frameset rows="20,*">
<frame>
<frame>
</frameset>
<frame>
</frameset>

</html>
```

Result:

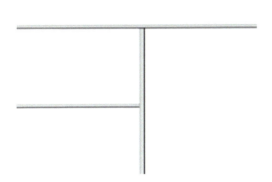

Creation of the "WEB1 HOME" file:

To put something inside the horizontal top band I created an html file called "WEB1 HOME".

In the sample I just added the paragraph with the name of the file to see the sentence **or paragraph** appear in that section.

But you could instead type: <frame src="WEB1 HOME.html"> as mentioned in the last code.

Note: any additional html file used as a source should be in the same folder or path of the main and original Frame coding.

```
<!DOCTYPE html>
<html>
<head>
<title>TEST</title>
</head>

<body bgcolor="blue">
<p>WEB1 HOME</P>

</html>
```

Result:

Frameset: "WEB2MAIN" code file using: target="Main section">Number 1,2 &3.

```
<!DOCTYPE html>
<html>
<head>
<title>TEST</title>
</head>

<body bgcolor="yellow">

<a href="nature-pictures.jpg" target="Main section">
        Number 1</a><br />
<a href="Hopetoun_falls.jpg" target="Main section">
        Number 2</a><br />
<a href="Bachalpseeflowers.jpg" target="Main section">
        Number 3</a><br />

</body>
</html>
```

Result:

Now we have 3 clickable links that leads to pictures saved in the same folder or path.

Number 1
Number 2
Number 3

Code including the "Main section" from "WEB2MAIN" code.

```
<!DOCTYPE html>
<html>
<head>
<title>TEST</title>
</head>

<frameset rows="70,*">
<frame src="FRAMESET WEB1 HOME.html">
<frameset cols="10%,90%">
<frameset rows="*,20%">
<frame src="FRAMESET WEB2MAIN .html">
<frame>
</frameset>
<frame name="Main section">
</frameset>
</frameset>

</html>
```

Result:

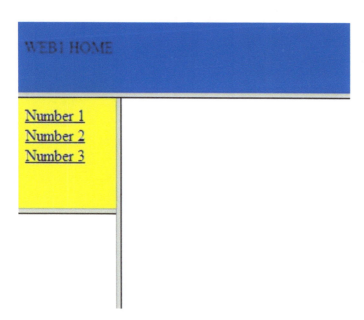

Check the Code to view these images in a green background on the right section of the screen

```
<!DOCTYPE html>
<html>
<head>
<title>TEST</title>
</head>

<body bgcolor="green">

Click on each number to view the images!

</body>
</html>
```

Result:

Click on each number to view the images!

Frameset add Contact email: Simple and clickable email contact.

```
<!DOCTYPE html>
<html>
<head>
<title>TEST</title>
</head>

<body bgcolor="black">

<a href="name@hotmail.com">Contact</a>

</body>
</html>
```

Result:

Frameset Tag: Has "WEB1 HOME<mark>.html</mark>" and "WEB2MAIN<mark>.html</mark>" files.

Please note:

If adding border="0" to frame, no frame border (line section).

If adding: scrolling="no" you cannot scroll.

And besides linking things inside, there are more attributes that you can add to frame.

Frameset code: view the whole screen:

```
<!DOCTYPE html>
<html>
<head>
<title>TEST</title>
</head>

<frameset rows="70,*">
<frame noresize src="FRAMESET WEB1 HOME.html">
<frameset cols="10%,90%">
<frameset rows="*,20%">
<frame scrolling="no" src="FRAMESET WEB2MAIN .html">
<frame src="Frameset add Contact email.html">
</frameset>
<frame src="VIEW Pictures.html" name="Main section">
</frameset>
</frameset>

</html>
```

Result:

WEB1 HOME

Number 1
Number 2
Number 3

Contact

Click on each number to view the images!

23. Conclusion:

The HTML is very simple to learn, by practicing the codes few times it becomes a simple routine, after that HTML can be used in a very confident way.

Practicing each code from this guide will help you understand each tag and its purpose and most importantly starting building your own website in no time.

ACKNOWLEDGMENTS

To You, dear readers for trying to learn coding in HTML.

www.ingramcontent.com/pod-product-compliance
Lightning Source LLC
Chambersburg PA
CBHW041144050326
40689CB00001B/471